A RIVER JOURNEY

The
Rhine

Ronan Foley

HODDER
Wayland

an imprint of Hodder Children's Books

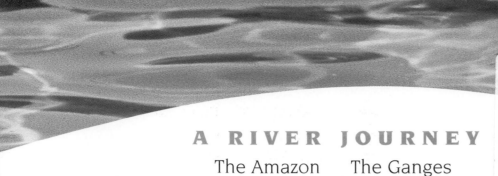

A RIVER JOURNEY

The Amazon   The Ganges
The Mississippi   The Nile
The Rhine   The Yangtze

For more information on this series and other Hodder Wayland titles, go to www.hodderwayland.co.uk

A *River Journey*: *The Rhine*

Copyright © 2003 Hodder Wayland
First published in 2003 by Hodder Wayland,
an imprint of Hodder Children's Books.

This paperback edition published in 2005

Commissioning Editor: Victoria Brooker   Cover design: Hodder Wayland   Book Design: Jane Hawkins
Book Editor: Deborah Fox   Picture Research: Shelley Noronha, Glass Onion Pictures
Book consultant: John Gerrard   Maps: Tony Fleetwood
Series consultant: Rob Bowden, EASI-Educational Resourcing

Series concept by: Environment and Society International –
Educational Resourcing

British Library Cataloguing in Publication Data
Foley, Ronan
 Rhine. - (A river journey)
 1. Rhine River - Juvenile literature 2. Rhine River -
Geography - Juvenile literature
 I. Title
 914.3'4
 ISBN 0750240423

Printed in China

Hodder Children's Books
A division of Hodder Headline Limited
338 Euston Road, London NW1 3BH

The website addresses (URLs) included in this book were valid at the time of going to press. However, because of the nature of the Internet, it is possible that some addresses may have changed, or sites may have changed or closed down since publication. While the author and Publisher regret any inconvenience this may cause readers, no responsibility for any such changes can be accepted by either the author or the Publisher.

The maps in this book use a conical projection, and so the indicator for North on the main map is only approximate.

Picture Acknowledgements

Cover: Bob Krist/Corbis; title page: Eye Ubiquitous; 3 Hodder Wayland Picture Library; 5 Skyscan; 6 Hugh Rooney/Eye Ubiquitous; 7 (left) David Cumming/Eye Ubiquitous (right) Richard Wagner/AKG Photo; 8 Bernd Ducke/Britstock-Ifa; 9 Eye Ubiquitous; 10 Skyscan; 11 (left) Topham, (right) Neil Egerton/Travel Ink, (bottom) Ray Roberts/Impact; 12 Skyscan; 13 James Davis; 14 Topham; 15 Bryan Pickering/Eye Ubiquitous; 16 Peter Siegenthaler/Britstock-Ifa; 17 Skyscan; 18 (left & right) Skyscan, 19 (left) Christophe Bluntzer/Impact, (right) James Davis; 19 (bottom) Jim McDonald/Corbis; 20 Popperfoto/Reuters; 21 (left) Skyscan, (right) Gerard Lacounette/Bios; 22 (left) Skyscan 4870, 22/23 (top) Gerard Lacounette/Bios; 23 Skyscan; 24 Stephen Coyne/Ecoscene; 24/25 James Davis; 26 Denis Bringard/Bios; 27 Bernd Ducke/Britstock-Ifa; 27 (bottom) Nick Weiseman/Eye Ubiquitous/Corbis; 28 Sally Morgan/Ecoscene; 29 David Cumming/Eye Ubiquitous; 30 Topham; 31 Bryan Pickering/Eye Ubiquitous, (top right) G. Graefenhain/Britstock-Ifa; 32 Robert Harding; 33 Popperfoto/Reuters; 34 Sally Morgan/Ecoscene; 35 Hodder Wayland Picture Library; 36 (top) Schmidbauer/Britstock-Ifa, (bottom) Skyscan; 37 Skyscan, (bottom right) Hodder Wayland Picture Library; 38 Robert Harding; 39 Geospace/Science Photo Library; 40 (left) Graham Kitching/Ecoscene; 40/41 Peter Palmer/Eye Ubiquitous; 41 (right) Larry Lee Photography/Corbis; 42 Mark Edwards/Still Pictures; 43 Robert Harding; 44 Mark Edwards/Still Pictures; 45 Anthony Cooper/Ecoscene.

Contents

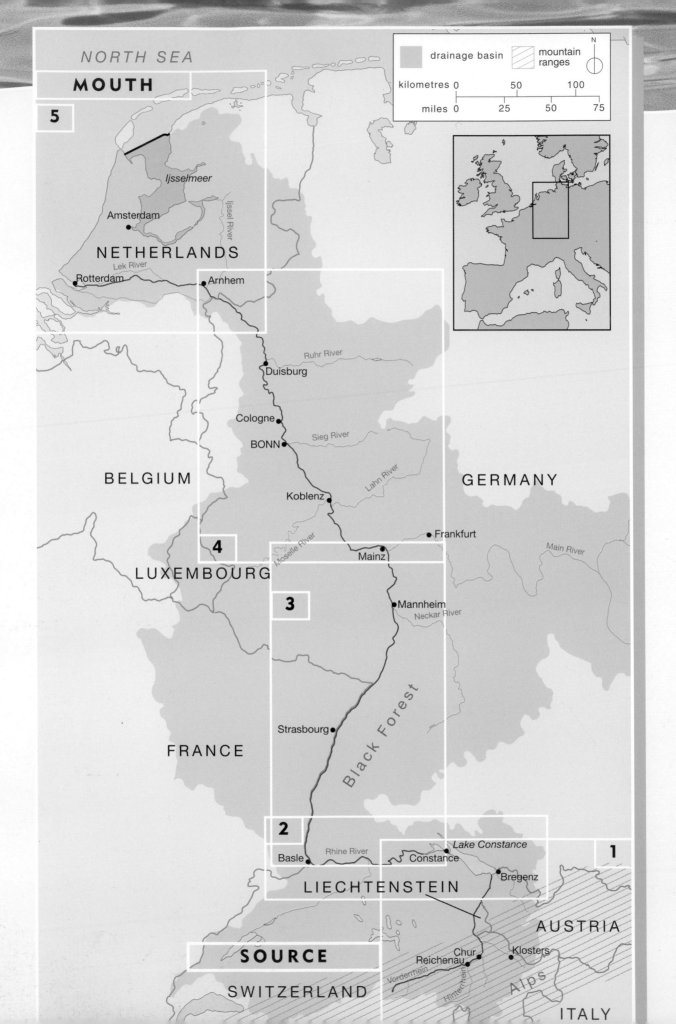

NORTH SEA

MOUTH

5

Ijsselmeer

Ijssel River

Amsterdam

NETHERLANDS

Lek River

Rotterdam

Arnhem

drainage basin

mountain ranges

kilometres 0 ⸻ 50 ⸻ 100

miles 0 — 25 — 50 — 75

N

Ruhr River

Duisburg

Cologne

BONN

Sieg River

BELGIUM

Lahn River

GERMANY

Koblenz

Frankfurt

4

Moselle River

Mainz

Main River

LUXEMBOURG

3

Mannheim

Neckar River

FRANCE

Strasbourg

Black Forest

2

Rhine River

Basle

Lake Constance

Constance

Bregenz

1

LIECHTENSTEIN

AUSTRIA

SOURCE

Chur

Klosters

Reichenau

SWITZERLAND

Vorderrhein

Hinterrhein

Alps

ITALY

Your Guide to the River

USING THEMED TEXT As you make your journey down the Rhine you will find topic headings about that area of the river. These symbols show what the text is about.

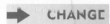 **NATURE** Plants, wildlife and the environment

HISTORY Events and people in the past

PEOPLE The lives and culture of local people

 **CHANGE** Things that have altered the area

ECONOMY Jobs and industry in the area

USING MAP REFERENCES Each chapter has a map that shows the section of the river we are visiting. The numbered boxes show exactly where a place of interest is located.

The Journey Ahead

The Rhine begins life as a stream from a lake high in the Swiss Alps. On its journey it crosses six countries and travels 1,320 kilometres to the North Sea. After thundering down mountainsides in Switzerland, the Rhine levels off as it flows through the tiny country of Liechtenstein. It then forms the border between Switzerland and Austria until it reaches the beautiful Lake Constance. It then winds its way to Basle from Lake Constance, forming the Swiss-German border in places.

The Rhine then heads towards the German cities of Mannheim and Mainz where it again forms a border – this time between France and Germany. At Mainz the river loops round again and heads into the classic Rhine countryside of steep-sided valleys, vineyards and castles. After flowing past Cologne, the river flows through the great industrial area of the Ruhr at Duisburg. When the Rhine crosses into Holland, it splits into several channels. They join together as the river completes its course near the great port and city of Rotterdam.

Let's start our river journey with a flight over the Swiss Alps and the source of the Rhine.

Map labels:
Lindau
Bregenz
km 0 — 50
m 0 — 25
LIECHTENSTEIN
Rhine River
Vaduz
AUSTRIA
SWITZERLAND
Klosters
Chur
Reichenau
Davos
Lake Tuma
Vorderrhein
Hinterrhein
Grisons
1
St Moritz

Below: The snow-capped Alps mark the beginning of the Rhine's long journey to the sea.

1. The Alpine Rhine

OUR JOURNEY BEGINS WITH A FLIGHT over the Rhine from its source in the Swiss mountains to the point at which it flows into Lake Constance. The turbulent river hurtles through the mountainous landscape below us. Natural hazards such as floods and landslides are common in this region. As the landscape flattens, the Rhine levels out and becomes a little calmer, but the river is still a powerful force. We see the first attempts to control the Rhine between the small country of Liechtenstein and Lake Constance, where we land and board a boat.

🐇 NATURE *Source of the Rhine*

Most people consider Lake Tuma to be the source of the Rhine, but some geographers claim there is an alternative source. They believe it is a tributary called the 'Hinterrhein' (meaning 'Back Rhine'), which begins life from the meltwaters of the Rheinwaldhorn Glacier MAP REF: 1. The glacier is the starting-point for the many streams and rivers that flow into the Rhine. But we will treat Lake Tuma as the start of our journey.

At a height of 2,345 metres, Lake Tuma is located in a valley carved out by glaciers during the last Ice Age over 10,000 years ago. The steep, mountainous walls rising around the lake are known as 'cirques'. The stream leaving Lake Tuma is the start of the Rhine, and at this point the river is known as 'Vorderrhein', which means 'Front Rhine'.

📖 HISTORY *The Rhinegold legend*

The headwaters of the Rhine are cloaked in history and legend. The most famous legend is German and is about gold! The story tells of an enormous amount of gold hidden in the mountains of the Rhine, fiercely guarded by the mountain people living there. The German composer Wagner used this legend as the inspiration for one of his famous operas written in 1869.

As well as gold, other metals have been found in the mountains of the Alpine Rhine and are still found today. Gold was always the most important, however, and it was used to make coins until the early eighteenth century.

Above: The Alphorn is a musical instrument unique to Switzerland. Musicians need a lot of room to play it!

pastures. Although very beautiful, life in these cold, rugged mountains is far from easy!

 NATURE *Mountain habitats*

The mountainous landscape is covered with snow and ice for several months each year, usually between November and March. Only the hardiest of plants and animals can survive such harsh conditions. One animal is the Chamois, a mountain goat. At one time the skin of the Chamois was used to produce an extremely soft leather. Now, though, the Chamois is a protected species.

As temperatures rise in the spring, the mountains come to life. Alpine plants such as the Swiss national flower, Edelweiss, suddenly appear. There are only a few hill farmers who live in this region. They graze goats and sheep on the fresh mountain

PEOPLE *Swiss languages*

The two mountain channels, the 'Vorderrhein' and the 'Hinterrhein', meet at Reichenau near the city of Chur. From this point the river is known simply as the Rhine. By the time we reach Reichenau, the Rhine has already fallen over a third of its total descent. The river flows through Switzerland and then north towards the tiny country of Liechtenstein.

Switzerland is famous for its watches, chocolate and even its cheese, but it is also known for the four languages spoken there! Three of them – French, German and Italian – are shared with their neighbouring countries, but Romansh, the fourth language, is almost uniquely Swiss. In fact, it is spoken by only about 50,000 people, who live mainly in the canton (meaning region) of Grisons in the Alpine Rhine valley. Romansh is a mixture of Latin and old French. Some words might sound familiar, such as 'bun di', which means 'good day', or 'cuppina', which means 'cup'.

$ ECONOMY *Liechtenstein's industry*

As we fly over Liechtenstein the Rhine starts to flatten and flow more slowly. Liechtenstein is only 160 square kilometres in size – ten times smaller than Greater London. It has a population of just 32,500 people, which makes it one of the smallest countries in the world.

The Rhine is important to Liechtenstein because it forms its border with Switzerland to the west. Its capital, Vaduz, sits on the eastern bank of the river, guarded by an impressive castle, which was built in the fourteenth century.

Today, Liechtenstein is an important economic centre. Banking is a major industry, employing around fifteen per cent of the workforce. More unusually, Liechtenstein also has a large dental industry due to the number of highly skilled dentists and dental technicians employed there. The people of Liechtenstein are wealthy and can afford good dental care. The country is the world's biggest exporter of false teeth!

Below: The capital of Liechtenstein, Vaduz, is overlooked by an impressive castle.

Taming the Rhine

Small dams or barrages were built across the river to cope with the changing water flow of the Rhine. Every year the spring meltwaters surge down the steep-sided valleys, carrying soil and rocks downstream. The barrages, including large metal nets, are designed to catch this debris and prevent it from damaging towns and villages further downstream. As the Rhine widens and slows, it begins to naturally deposit its rocks in and alongside the river.

From Liechtenstein onwards, flooding used to cause huge problems. The land was quite flat and for hundreds of years the Rhine would frequently burst its banks during the spring. To protect residents and valuable farmland from the floods, the river was 'channelized' in the early nineteenth century. When a river is channelized, it is forced to flow between raised embankments instead of flooding on to the surrounding land. But rivers are a powerful force. Some geographers believe that, over time, a river will resist such change and will try to return to its natural course. If the Rhine were to burst its artificial embankments, water would surge on to the surrounding land very rapidly.

Below: This channel in Liechtenstein controls and straightens the course of the river. The stones reinforce the riverbanks.

Above: The Cresta Run is a famous bobsleigh course. It was created by the British in 1885.
Left: Davos in Switzerland is one of many winter resorts that attract thousands of tourists.

✋ PEOPLE *Mountain livelihoods*

Traditional mountain livelihoods are rapidly disappearing. At one time people would have made a living from farming and hunting wild animals. Today, people are finding new ways to earn their living.

Tourism is the most important source of income in the mountain regions of Grisons and Ticino. In the summer the mountains are popular with walkers and climbers, but winter sports, such as skiing and snow-boarding, attract the most visitors.

Some of the ski resorts, such as Davos and Klosters, are world famous. They are located on tributaries of the Rhine. There is also a well-known bobsleigh run, known as the Cresta Run, near the town of St Moritz.

Tourism in Switzerland employs around 350,000 people, though many of these jobs are seasonal. In the Alpine Rhine region, where skiing accounts for about seventy per cent of tourism, local people may have several jobs throughout the year. They work as ski instructors during the winter season and as mountain guides during the summer. In autumn they rest or help prepare the resort for the next season!

After landing, we transfer to a lake steamer to continue our journey across the beautiful Lake Constance.

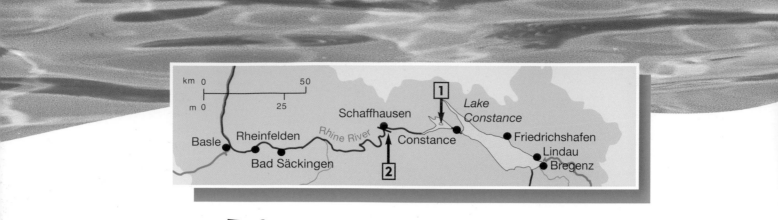

2. The Upper Rhine

AFTER CROSSING LAKE CONSTANCE we board a smaller boat that will take us to the spectacular Rhine Falls. Below the falls, we return to the river, which is now safe for boats to navigate for the rest of its course. From Rheinfelden, we begin to see the importance of the Rhine for commercial river traffic. By the time we reach Basle we have descended a further 150 metres through the slow meanders of the Rhine that form the border between Switzerland and Germany.

Below: The muddy river Rhine tumbles into the light blue water of Lake Constance near the town of Bregenz.

Right: The walled town of Lindau is a popular tourist destination. This tourist cruise boat is about to explore Lake Constance.

NATURE *River to lake*

The Rhine enters Lake Constance near Bregenz in a rather unusual way, which is easier to see from the air. The muddy river tumbles into the clear blue lake in a long stream of water, like a short canal. The effect is like a waterfall, but under water. It happens when the river water, which is filled with heavy sediment, meets the sediment-free lake water. This feature is known locally as the 'Rheinbrech'. The Rhine merges with the lake, emerging again as a river sixty-five kilometres to the west to continue its journey downstream.

$ ECONOMY *Lake Constance & tourism*

Lake Constance is the largest lake in Germany, even though it is shared with Switzerland and Austria. Known to German speakers as 'Bodensee', Lake Constance is surrounded by rolling hills and picturesque towns, particularly on the German side of the lake. It is very popular with tourists, and the tourist industry here supports hundreds of jobs. Over 170,000 tourists a year visit the city of Constance, with at least eighty per cent of them coming from within Germany itself. Constance actually stretches across the German border into Switzerland and is therefore a city in two countries!

Many visitors take a boat trip on the lake, but they also come to visit the local towns and cities. Of particular interest is the walled town of Lindau. It stands on an island connected to the mainland by a bridge and a causeway.

Our steamer stops at Reichenau Island MAP REF: 1 where we visit St George's Church, one of the lake's most popular attractions. It is famous for its frescoes, or wall paintings, that date back as far as the ninth century. Whilst the sights of Lake Constance are indeed beautiful, other people come here just to enjoy the clean mountain air, particularly during the warm and bright summers.

The Zeppelins

On the northern shore of Lake Constance is Friedrichshafen, a town famous as the home of giant airships known as 'Zeppelins'. A German nobleman called Ferdinand Graf von Zeppelin invented these enormous airships. The first flight of a Zeppelin, the LZ1, took place over Lake Constance on 2 July 1900. A total of 119 Zeppelins, each the length of two football pitches, were built in Friedrichshafen between 1900 and 1938.

During the First World War, Germans used Zeppelins to drop bombs on England. After the war they were used mainly for luxury air travel. In 1929, the 'Graf Zeppelin' (also known as LZ127) left Lake Constance to fly around the world, stopping in New York, Tokyo and Los Angeles before returning to the lake.

In May 1937, a Zeppelin called the 'Hindenburg' caught fire as it came in to land at Lakehurst, New Jersey in the USA. The reason it exploded was because the silver paint used on the airship was highly flammable. The balloon was filled with hydrogen gas and this, combined with an electrical discharge from the silver paint, caused the airship to rapidly catch fire. Because of passengers' fears following this disaster, Zeppelins were no longer built.

In 2000, however, a New Technology Zeppelin was successfully launched in Friedrichshafen to celebrate the Zeppelin's hundredth birthday.

Below: The first Zeppelin makes its maiden voyage over Lake Constance in July 1900.

NATURE *The Rhine Falls*

About twenty kilometres after leaving Lake Constance, the Rhine meets another major obstacle – the Rhine Falls [MAP REF: 2] at Schaffhausen. The river suddenly speeds up as it is forced through a 150 metre-wide gorge before plunging vertically for twenty-three metres as a thundering, foaming mass of white water. The Rhine Falls are a popular tourist site. They attracted over 1.5 million visitors in 2000.

Depending on the time of year, between 700 to 1,080 cubic metres of water plunge over the falls every second. That is equivalent to filling about twenty Olympic-sized swimming pools every minute! The

Above: Tourists get a closer look at the Rhine Falls from the viewing station on the right of the photograph.

falls reach their peak flow during the spring when the mountain snow melts and swells the river system.

Waterfalls are normally found where rivers meet hard rocks – in this case limestone – that are difficult to erode. As the softer rock downstream continues to erode, the river bed falls away and creates the sudden drop in the river. This process usually takes many thousands of years. Geologists believe that the Rhine Falls were formed about 15,000 years ago. They are a classic example of a waterfall.

→ CHANGE *A great waterway*

The Rhine carries more river traffic than any other waterway in the world. In 2001 an estimated 200 million tonnes of cargo were transported on the river, which is equivalent to the amount carried by 366,000 articulated lorries! This is twice as much cargo as is carried on the river Seine in France and almost four times as much as the river Danube of Central Europe.

Despite its importance as a waterway, the Rhine is not fully navigable until the town of Rheinfelden, about 50 kilometres downstream of the Rhine Falls. This is because the higher Rhine is too dangerous for large boats. Between the Rhine Falls and Rheinfelden the river is blocked by a series of dams. Originally planners had hoped to make the Rhine navigable upstream as far as Constance. This aim was never achieved, but river journeys on the Rhine are still measured from Constance where a bridge over the Rhine marks 'kilometre zero'. This means that our boat journey starts 149 kilometres further west at Rheinfelden.

As part of a network of European waterways, the Rhine is now joined to the Danube by a canal near Nürnberg. The

Above: The best way to explore the Rhine is by boat. This large speedboat carries tourists down the river.

Rhine-Main-Danube Canal was completed in 1992. It is an important trade route for ships sailing between the Atlantic Ocean and the Black Sea.

$ ECONOMY *Powering the way*

At the turn of the twentieth century, European scientists were experimenting with methods of generating electricity. One of their challenges was to find out how to capture the enormous power needed to turn the generators to create electricity. They soon turned to the Rhine for their answer. The fast-flowing water provided a constant and free source of power that could be used to turn the generators as it flowed downstream. This hydroelectric power (HEP) was first developed at Rheinfelden in 1898, with the building of Europe's first HEP plant. Other power stations have since been built on many of the fast-flowing tributaries that tumble down from the Alps and the mountains surrounding the

Black Forest. The tributaries are ideal for generating HEP. Even though they are smaller than the Rhine's main tributaries, their steep gradient gives the water greater power.

 NATURE *Water into energy*

The water needed to generate HEP is normally stored behind a dam across a valley. It is then released to power the generators. Storing the water in this way has the added benefit of controlling flooding because water can be released slowly over time.

HEP is also beneficial for the environment, because it produces electricity without the harmful emissions of other methods, such as coal or gas-fired power stations. As global warming becomes a concern for everyone, clean forms of energy such as HEP will become increasingly important.

Below: The hydroelectric plant in the bottom left of the photograph is over one hundred years old. It was the first of its type to be built in Europe.

📖 HISTORY *Historic towns & abbeys*

We pass a number of historic sites along the peaceful River Rhine between Schaffhausen and Basle. At Rheinau a Benedictine Abbey, built in 1705, juts into the river on a small peninsula of land that is actually in Switzerland. Fifty kilometres upstream of Schaffhausen we pass under a bridge in the town of Bad Säckingen. This was one of the first bridges built over the Rhine, sometime between 1570 and 1620. As we stop for a quick tour you can see that the bridge, and the town, are still very well preserved. The bridge itself is covered and spans over 200 metres across the river. A white line in the middle marks the German-Swiss border.

As we approach Basle we pass the town of Kaiseraugst. In 1982 an important discovery of Roman treasure was made at an old Roman town close to Kaiseraugst called 'Augusta Raurica'. Although the town was abandoned hundreds of years ago, a smaller Roman settlement called 'Basilea'

Above left: Bad Säckingen has one of the best-preserved wooden bridges on the Rhine. It took fifty years to build during the sixteenth century. Above: Germany, France and Switzerland meet at this precise point in the middle of the river.

survived much better. Located across the river, that is our next stop. Today the town is much bigger and is known by its modern name, Basle.

✋ PEOPLE *Carnival in Basle*

The Swiss city of Basle marks an important turning point in the river. The Rhine suddenly heads north. A large post standing in the middle of the river marks another interesting feature of the Rhine at Basle. It shows the exact point where the countries of France, Switzerland and Germany meet.

Basle itself is a beautifully preserved city. It feels quite different to surrounding towns and many local people even speak their own dialect of German, mixed in with a bit of French!

Above: By the time it reaches Basle, the River Rhine has become quite wide and can be used by larger vessels. Left: The festival of 'Fassnacht' is a huge celebration. The colourful costumes and music here in Basle are typical of the event.

Basle is famous for its Carnival or 'Fassnacht'. It is held for three days in the week after Ash Wednesday, usually towards the end of February. Throughout Europe and in Germany in particular, festivals or carnivals are held during January and February. It is a tradition going back over two thousand years. It allowed people to release their energy before the fasting period of Lent.

Basle's 'Fassnacht' has street processions, colourful costumes, public entertainment and music. Groups of people, known as 'cliques', dress up in historic costumes and parade through the city streets at night with elaborate decorative lanterns to light their path.

We board one of the large industrial barges at Basle harbour for the next stage of our journey.

Map labels: Mainz, Worms, Mannheim, Ludwigshafen, Heidelberg, GERMANY, Speyer, Neckar River, Main River, Karlsruhe, Baden-Baden, FRANCE, Black Forest, Strasbourg, Rhine River, Vosges Mountains, km 0 50, m 0 25, 1 Basle, Rheinfelden

3. Controlling the Rhine

LEAVING BASLE WE ENTER A section of the Rhine that has been drastically changed by human actions. These changes mean that the river flows more slowly than before and its course has been raised above the surrounding countryside. It runs in almost a straight line along a wide valley separating the Black Forest to the east and the French Vosges Mountains to the west. We pass the French city of Strasbourg, before winding our way north to the industrial city of Mannheim and the historic city of Mainz.

Below: The ultra-modern Louise Weiss building became the new home of the European Parliament in 1999.

FRANCE
100 m

FERMETURE POSSIBLE
SANS PREAVIS POUR
RAISONS DE SECURITE

SCHLIESSUNG AUS
SICHERHEITSGRÜNDEN
OHNE HINWEIS MÖGLICH

Above: The river widens to 100 metres near the town of Gerstheim, with France on the left and Germany on the right of the picture. Left: A border-crossing gate shows the EU flag with a warning in German and French that the gate will be closed in emergencies!

📖 HISTORY *The river as a border*

Rivers are important physical boundaries. On many maps, national borders are drawn down the centre of rivers. The Rhine forms a long-standing natural boundary between Germany and France. In this section of the river you need to speak French if you get off on the west bank, but German if you choose the eastern bank! In the past, battles between France and Germany mean that national borders have shifted. Between 1870 and 1919 for example, much of Alsace-Lorraine, the French region to the west of the Rhine, was German. After the First World War, it became part of France again.

In 1979, the city of Strasbourg, 140 kilometres downstream of Basle, was chosen as the home of the European Parliament, the governing body of the European Union (EU). This decision reflected the strong links between two of the Union's most important countries – France and Germany. Indeed France and Germany were two of the six original members of the EU, so it is perhaps no surprise that they located their headquarters on the Rhine. Since January 2002, the two countries, along with ten other European states, have shared the same currency – the euro.

$ ECONOMY   *Industrial heartland*

The Rhine and its tributaries flow through the industrial heartland of Western Europe and so its waterways have long been a natural transport link. Today, many goods are carried by road, but the river remains an important method of transport for large and bulky cargoes, including coal, grain, timber, oil, chemicals and iron ore. By using the river, industries can move vast amounts of material. Barges can be up to one hundred metres long – the length of a football pitch – and hold up to 3,000 tonnes of grain or coal. To transport the same amount by train would require fifteen large rail carriages, and by road at least fifty large lorries!

Transporting goods in such bulk is cheaper than by rail or road. It also uses fuel more efficiently, which is better for the environment. Of course the journey is slower by river (by around ten times in fact), so journeys must be planned well in advance to make sure goods arrive on schedule.

➡ CHANGE   *Rhine shipping canal*

River channels change and shift naturally. They form meanders by eroding material on one bank, where the river flows fast, and depositing it on the other, where it slows down. The bottom of the river channel also changes shape and depth because material from higher up the river is deposited where the river slows down and widens out into a level valley.

North of Basle the river's natural course has been changed to overcome the problems of deposition and erosion, which change the shape and depth of the river. Because river traffic is so important to the

Above: Huge barges pass each other as they carry cargo up and down the river.

economy, the river has to be deep and wide enough for large ships to pass through. To form a controlled shipping canal, a channel is built between raised banks called 'levees'. The canal actually sits a few metres above the surrounding land. The old route of the river – the 'ResteRhein' MAP REF: 1 or 'The Spare Rhine' – is below us and is now only used as an overflow channel for the main canal. The ship canal is controlled by locks that raise and lower the level of water in the 'new' channel. This ensures that there is always enough water to keep the larger boats afloat. By managing the river in this way, it is also possible to prevent local flooding.

Between Rheinfelden and close to Baden-Baden, 170 kilometres further downstream, there are twelve enormous locks that control the Rhine.

Left: At Kembs the channels, locks and dams on the right highlight how humans have controlled the flow of the Rhine. The old winding river channel is on the left
Below: After the Rhine was channelized, the old river channels have become quiet backwaters rich in plant and animal life.

Above: Nuclear power stations are a familiar sight on the Rhine between Basle and Strasbourg, particularly on the French side of the Rhine.

$ ECONOMY *Nuclear power*

Nuclear power stations are a common feature along the Rhine, especially on the western, French side of the river. Nuclear power stations need large quantities of water to cool down the equipment used to generate electricity. This makes the Rhine valley an ideal site for generating nuclear power.

The power stations have been built alongside the Rhine. They are linked to the river by small canals. Seventy-six per cent of France's electricity is generated by nuclear power – more than in any other European country. In 1999, there were nineteen power stations on the German side of the river providing thirty per cent of the country's electricity. They are slowly being closed down, however, as nuclear power is becoming less popular in Germany. People there are worried about the dangers of radiation from potential nuclear accidents.

 NATURE **A natural treasure**

To the right of our barge are the rolling hills and forests of the Black Forest. This is one of the most scenic and popular areas of Germany. It runs all the way from the Swiss border to the area near the cities of Karlsruhe and Stuttgart. Much of the region is covered in coniferous trees such as spruce and pine, and there are approximately 23,000 kilometres of forest trails open to walkers and cyclists.

The Black Forest lies within the German state of Baden-Württemberg and the state takes an active role in conservation. Development within the forest is strictly

controlled in order to preserve this natural treasure for future generations.

Look out for a tall spire rising above the horizon. This is the 116-metre spire of the beautiful Freiburger Münster cathedral in Freiburg-im-Breisgau, the capital of the Black Forest region.

$ ECONOMY *Clocks and cakes*

Agriculture and paper-making are important industries in the Black Forest region, but a more unusual local industry is clock-making. There is even a local tour people can take called 'the Route of Clocks'. As well as traditional agricultural crops, such as potatoes and grain, the mild climate allows farmers to grow ornamental plants, hops (for brewing) and tobacco.

The Black Forest is also well known for its fine foods, many of which are exported around the world. These include the world famous Black Forest Gateau, a delicious cake made with chocolate, cream and cherries. It is very rich though, so if you are offered some, don't eat too much!

Main picture: Many small tributaries flow into the river from the rolling hills of the Black Forest, which runs along the eastern bank of the Rhine.

NATURE *A poisonous brew*

Like many large industrial rivers, the Rhine has a long history of pollution. Since the start of the Industrial Revolution in the early nineteenth century, the Rhine has been used as a dumping ground for untreated waste from town sewage systems and from industries such as paper-making and chemical manufacture. In less than 200 years the Rhine has been turned into a poisonous brew. Local species such as the Rhine salmon were completely extinct by 1940. The construction of canals, locks and weirs has also disrupted the natural habitat, threatening any species that might have survived the pollution.

CHANGE *Cleaning up its act?*

One of the most serious pollution incidents on the Rhine took place in 1986 when a fire at a chemical factory north of Basle released thirty tonnes of pesticides, chemical dyes and fungicides into the river. As a result, river life died up to 150 kilometres downstream. In 1987, following this incident, the six countries through which the Rhine flows announced a major clean-up campaign to reduce pollution. New laws control the amount of waste that is dumped into the river and regular monitoring is slowly helping to restore life in parts of the Rhine. Switzerland, Germany and France now work together in Basle to keep the river clean.

Just across the border, in Germany, a monitoring station pumps water from the river and checks its quality every six minutes, twenty-four hours a day. Industries that pollute the river can be traced and fined.

Salmon have now been re-introduced to the Rhine. By 1998 they had been seen as far upstream as Strasbourg – an encouraging sign that the Rhine is at last cleaning up its act!

Below: The salmon ladder is the series of small steps on the left of the photograph. Salmon swim upstream by jumping from pool to pool up the ladder, bypassing bigger obstacles in the main river channel.

HISTORY   *Bells of the Rhine*

About 50 kilometres north of Strasbourg the Rhine again flows through a single country – Germany. Throughout the world, rivers are a natural point for the location of towns, and along this stretch of the Rhine we pass many of Germany's oldest towns. Several of them are famous for their ancient cathedrals. It is not uncommon to hear bells ringing as you pass through towns

Above: Heidelberg is a famous University town on a tributary of the Rhine. It has many historical buildings and is a popular tourist destination.

such as Worms, Speyer or Mainz. The cathedral at Worms is one of the oldest. It was first built in AD 1000. Worms cathedral was made famous by Martin Luther, the founder of the Protestant faith. He founded this faith in 1517 after attending a religious meeting at Worms.

At Mainz, we leave our barge and board a hydrofoil that will take us quickly through the Rhine Gorge.

Arnhem
Emmerich
3 → Wesel
Dortmund
Duisburg
Ruhr River

GERMANY

km 0   50
m 0   25

Cologne
Sieg River
BONN
Lahn River
Koblenz
Moselle River
Boppard
2 →
Mainz
Frankfurt
Main River
1 →

THE NEXT STAGE OF OUR JOURNEY takes us through the classic Rhine landscape of steep-sided valleys, crowded with vineyards and dotted with historic towns. After leaving the Rhine Gorge, we approach the Ruhr, a major industrial centre. The Rhine is here joined by some of its biggest tributaries. They increase the amount of water in the river, which can make it extremely dangerous … it's a good thing the captain knows the waters well!

Below: The broad river Rhine flows through a typical valley with steep-sided hills and small picturesque towns squeezed along the riverbanks.

Above: The Rhine Gorge is a major wine-growing area. Vineyards line the steep banks above the river.

 NATURE *The Rhine Gorge*

As we travel north on our hydrofoil the river meanders past Mainz, heading slightly west before turning north again. The river then enters the Rhine Gorge MAP REF: 1 . The gorge was formed thousands of years ago when the river arrived at an area of very hard volcanic rocks. The river found an area of weakness in the slate rocks and, over time, eroded a channel through this weaker section. This became the deep gorge surrounded by steep mountains and hills that we see today.

Look how narrow the Rhine Gorge is. It is only as wide as the river that flows through it. This is because the rate at which the river cuts into the rock is far greater than the rate at which the sides erode to form a normal, V-shaped valley. We can see this very clearly as we travel north towards Bonn.

 NATURE *Rhine vines*

Most of Germany's vineyards owe their existence to the Rhine. The valleys of the Rhine Gorge are lined with wine-producing vineyards. This area of the river is ideal for vines because the sunny, steep, south-facing slopes and well-drained soils produce ideal growing conditions for them.

In 2000 Germany was the sixth biggest wine exporter in the world. In 1997, a total of 97,900 hectares of land along the Rhine and its tributaries was used for cultivating vines. This accounts for ninety-four per cent of the total wine-growing land in Germany. Two-thirds of the wine-growing areas in the Rhine are very small vineyards of less than thirty hectares. Most of the wines produced are white. Because Germany is quite far north, the colder climate is better for growing white grapes. A high proportion of the German wine that is exported is of only medium quality. Many of the best wines are only found inside Germany.

$ ECONOMY *The tourist trail*

Our hydrofoil can travel at speeds of up to 65 kilometres an hour. It is possible to travel from Mainz to Cologne and back again – a distance of 300 kilometres – in just half a day. This fast transport link has opened up this section of the river to large numbers of visitors, many of whom never see the rest of the Rhine at all. Several companies run package tours through the Rhine Gorge, stopping off for lunch or to visit a castle or vineyard on the way.

Tourism here has a long history. The first tourist steamships were in operation as far back as 1826. The largest side-wheeled paddle steamer in the world, the 'Goethe', is still in service, though it is the last one left on the German section of the Rhine.

Below: The side-wheeled paddle steamer, the 'Goethe', has carried sightseers along the Rhine since 1826. Right: The Lorelei Rock towers over the Rhine at St Goarshausen. It is the most famous landmark on our journey. Right top: The 'Rhine in Flames' is a spectacular summer festival watched by over half a million people every August.

HISTORY *Legend of the Lorelei*

As we wind our way around a long bend near Bingen, we enter one of the most exciting stretches of the Rhine – the Lorelei Valley. Romantic castle ruins, such as Stahleck and fortress Schönburg near Oberwesel, tower over us. At St Goarshausen we reach Lorelei Rock MAP REF: 2, one of the region's key tourist attractions. This is one of the most dangerous parts of our journey due to the shifting river currents.

The Lorelei Rock is 133 metres high. Legend has it that it was the home of a beautiful woman whose songs lured unsuspecting sailors to their deaths on the dangerous river shallows underneath. The 'Lorelei-Lied' (Lorelei Song) is one of the most famous songs in Germany.

PEOPLE *The Rhine in Flames*

In August the spectacular 'Rhine in Flames' festivals take place. The dramatic shows originally started in Koblenz in 1766. They

were organized by the ruling classes of the time, but they had died out by the end of the nineteenth century because the government had decided that they were too expensive. In 1956 the festivals were started again to attract tourists to the area after the Second World War.

The festivals come to life along the stretch of the river between Boppard and Bonn. In the biggest 'Rhine in Flames' festival, six towns along this part of the river 'burn' as a flotilla of eighty ships sails past. To re-create the 'burnings', houses and restaurants along both banks of the Rhine place red lights in their windows and on their terraces. Giant flares are set off near the castles, churches and historic buildings – the red glow of the flares and the heavy smoke make the fires look real. The flotilla sails for seventeen kilometres down the Rhine. Around 30,000 people watch from the ships and another 500,000 line the banks of the river.

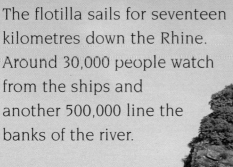

 NATURE *Tributaries of the Rhine*

As we speed downstream from Boppard you will notice more tributaries entering the Rhine. They are larger than the ones we saw further upstream. The River Main joined the Rhine at Mainz having started its journey over 524 kilometres away near Bayreuth in eastern Germany. At Koblenz we are joined by the Moselle river, which started life in the Vosges Mountains in France, about 515 kilometres to the south. Smaller, but still important, tributaries such as the Lahn and the Sieg, join from the east. Many of these tributaries are carefully managed to prevent flooding. A number of dams and reservoirs regulate the amount of water flowing into the Rhine.

Above: The point at which the clear River Moselle joins the murky Rhine at Koblenz is known as the 'Deutsches Eck' (German Corner). The two rivers are quite different in colour.

 NATURE *Living with risk*

Despite efforts at controlling floods along the river, nature is still a powerful force, especially on a river as large as the Rhine. During periods of heavy rainfall the tributaries increase the amount of water in the main river channel, which often causes flooding.

The cathedral city of Cologne and other towns and agricultural areas nearby are regularly affected. Severe flooding took

Above: Regular flooding causes extensive damage in riverside cities like Cologne. This picture was taken after torrential rain in January 1995.

place in the area four times during the 1990s. The flood of 1993 was the worst ever – the river was 10.63 metres above its normal level. Five people were killed and 10,000 litres of heating oil from homes and factories leaked into the floodwaters. In the suburb of Rodenkirchen, which was badly affected by the floods, residents protested and persuaded the city government to extend flood protection to their homes. Portable flood barriers were introduced, which prevented further damage to homes during a flood in 1999.

Despite the improvements in flood protection, the Rhine is still an unpredictable river and even the best barriers might not prevent flooding in the future.

PEOPLE *Carnival time again*

At the end of February there are five exciting days of busy Carnival celebrations in Cologne. One of the festival days is dedicated to women who have the freedom to play pranks on men, such as cutting off their ties!

The highlight of the Carnival is the last day, 'Rosenmontag'. The name comes from the German word, 'rasen', which means to rave or run amok. A big procession takes place when huge carnival figures are paraded along the streets. Floats are decorated with figures celebrating historical, political and legendary events and there are over a hundred bands playing music. Horse-drawn carriages pass through streets crammed with hundreds of thousands of cheering people. The procession in 2002 covered 6.5 kilometres and lasted for over three hours.

Left: The river is a major transport route for cargoes of coal, plastic and other goods seen here loaded on to barges at Duisburg.

➡ CHANGE *Inland ports*

The Rhine is the main transport waterway of Western Europe. River traffic has been toll-free since 1816. In this section of the river, between Mainz and the Ruhr, over 110 million tonnes of cargo are transported each year. North of Cologne large barges and motor-steamers carry iron ore, petrol, oil, coal and grain to the Ruhr and Rotterdam. We will also see push barges, or tugs, pushing up to six barges that are joined together.

Most vessels stop at the 'Duisport' in Duisburg, the largest inland port in the world. It developed when the small boats carrying coal from the Ruhr area to the east needed to find a place to transfer their cargoes on to the bigger Rhine boats. These larger boats are cheaper to run, but, because of their size, can only sail on the main river channel. Duisport harbour covers an area of 1,000 hectares (the size of almost 2,000 football pitches) and handles about fifty million tonnes of cargo every year.

$ ECONOMY *The Ruhr District*

As we pass Duisburg, to the east is one of the most important concentrations of industry in Western

Above: Though small, this tug can push six fully loaded barges in front of it.

Europe, known as the 'Ruhrgebiet', or Ruhr District. It is named after a tributary of the Rhine. It first developed during the Industrial Revolution of the early nineteenth century at the point where the two rivers, the Rhine and the Ruhr, meet. A number of towns – Essen, Duisburg, Dortmund and Gelsenkirchen – developed around huge iron, coal and steel works. This urban area, known as a conurbation, has a combined population of over five million people. The river barges still carry large loads of iron, coal and steel today, proving how important the Rhine remains to the economies of the region. The Ruhr District alone produces thirty-one per cent of the European Union's coal and eleven per cent of its steel.

The district is changing though as minerals such as coal become scarce. People prefer cleaner and safer fuels and industries. New industries such as mechanical engineering and high-tech computing are providing new opportunities as the coal industry and other traditional industries decline.

PEOPLE *Enjoying the river*

Between Duisburg and the Dutch border, we pass close to the towns of Kleve and Wesel in the area known as 'Unterer Niederrhein' (Under Lower Rhine) **MAP REF: 3** in the Rhine floodplain. About forty per cent of the area is set aside as a nature reserve. It covers 25,000 hectares, most of which is wetland. This means it qualifies as a 'Ramsar' site – Ramsar is an international agreement that recognizes and protects important wetland areas. The reserve includes several different protected areas. It is an excellent place to go bird-watching for green-winged teal, tufted duck, lapwing, golden plovers, great crested grebes, black-tailed godwits and reed warblers.

The nature reserve includes large areas of flooded gravel pits and open riverbanks with sand and pebble shores. Many recreational activities are found here, such as sailing, motor-boating, wind-surfing, swimming, fishing and camping.

NATURE *Agriculture*

Some of the main crops grown in this part of the Rhine include maize, tobacco, sugar beet and vegetables. The downside of this agricultural activity is that farmers use large amounts of fertilizer to try and increase crop yields. Over time the fertilizers build

Above: The spraying of agricultural land with chemicals near rivers has serious environmental implications. Fertilizers are washed off the land and pollute the river water.

up in the soils and plant life, and they can also run off the fields and find their way into the Rhine and other rivers. In fact agricultural chemicals (and especially fertilizers) are the main source of pollution on the Rhine.

The water quality of the river is affected and the chemicals can harm, and even kill, fish and plants. This is because the nutrients contained in the fertilizers encourage the growth of tiny aquatic (water-based) plants called algae. If the algae grow at a faster rate than the fish living in the river can eat it, large mats of algae form on the surface of the river. This process stops the sunlight from reaching the algae underneath. Without sunlight, the algae die and begin to rot. This process, called 'eutrophication', starves the water of oxygen, and without oxygen fish and other aquatic animals die.

Today the Rhine is better protected from pollution by European Union laws on clean water. These laws cannot stop all pollution however, as the pollutants can travel great distances in groundwater or can suddenly be washed into rivers during heavy rains. This means some fertilizers will always get into the Rhine. The best solution would be for farmers to stop using agricultural chemicals by switching to organic farming.

We board a large ocean-going cargo vessel at Emmerich. We can follow the main river channel into the Rhine Delta in the Netherlands.

Below: The Rhine splits into many separate channels as it enters the Netherlands. They are all linked by canals.

5. The Rhine estuary

THE COURSE OF THE Rhine becomes complicated as it nears the sea. Its delta has many separate channels that run into the sea at different places along the coast. As we criss-cross this landscape of windmills and canals, it becomes hard to work out exactly where we are on the river! We stick to what most people consider the main channel, which passes Rotterdam and the huge 'Europoort' before entering the North Sea.

📖 HISTORY *War in the Netherlands*

During the Second World War, the river channels in the Netherlands and northern Germany were of great military importance. As the German army was forced out of France by the Allied (American and British) Forces in 1944, fierce battles were fought to capture important bridges over the Rhine at Nijmegen and Arnhem. We pass under one of these bridges as we travel past the town of Arnhem. The Germans blew up the bridges after crossing them to slow down the Allies. The Allies were in a constant race to capture the bridges before the Germans destroyed them. Several of these battles have been made into films such as 'A Bridge Too Far' and 'Saving Private Ryan'.

🐇 NATURE *Dutch river channels*

In the delta region, the flow of water slows down as the Rhine reaches the flat land near the sea. As it slows, the river begins to deposit the sediment it is carrying and causes the river to spread out and split into several channels. This happens to the Rhine as it reaches the Netherlands. As the river splits a number of new channels are formed, each with a different name. The main channels, through which about two-thirds of the water flows, are called the Lek and the Waal. The Lek continues west to Rotterdam and enters the North Sea at Hoek van Holland (Hook of Holland). The Waal also flows west and merges with other smaller tributaries to form the

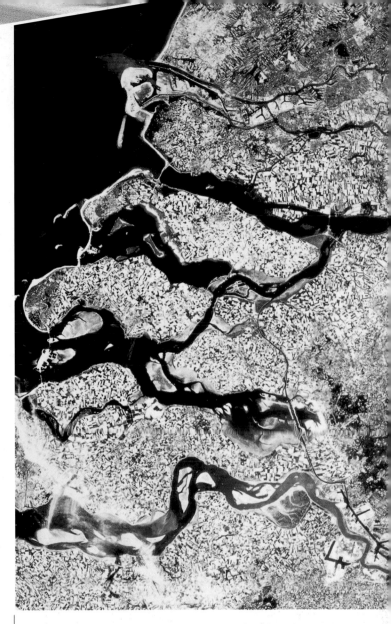

Above: This satellite image of the Rhine estuary shows some of the channels as they reach the sea. The Lek is the most northerly channel you can see.

Hollandschdiep, an arm of the North Sea. A third channel, known as the Crooked Rhine, leads to Utrecht and continues west to the sea as the Old Rhine.

All the channels are part of the river's delta system and stretch from north of Amsterdam to as far south as Antwerp in Belgium. We will follow the Lek, which most people consider to be the main channel through the delta region.

NATURE *Taking on nature*

The river channels of the delta are also affected by the fact that most of the Netherlands' land is very low-lying. About twenty-four per cent of the country is below sea level and this makes it very vulnerable to flooding by the sea. Much of the Rhine delta includes land that has been reclaimed from the sea over the centuries. The sea is kept out by building high sea walls. Although the sea must be kept out to keep the land dry and the water fresh, the Rhine needs to reach the sea too.

In the past few years the Rhine and other rivers in the area have suffered extremely high water levels due to high rainfall. In 1995 rivers reached unexpected heights and breached the dams – known locally as dykes – which flooded agricultural land and several towns. To avoid such problems, dykes are being relocated and water meadows lowered. This allows rivers to flow more freely with fewer obstacles along their course. The water meadows also provide a natural floodplain for excess water.

$ ECONOMY *Tulips from Amsterdam*

Agriculture is very important in the delta area. Flower-growing creates a lot of jobs and money for the Netherlands, which produces around nine billion flower bulbs every year. About seven billion are exported. This earned the country £2.5 billion in 2000.

Left: All along the Dutch coast, giant dykes like this one at Afsluitdijk stop the sea from flooding the low-lying land. The sea is on the right of this picture. Below: Flower-growing, especially of tulips, is a major industry in the delta area and every spare piece of land is used.

The most popular bulbs produced, and the ones the Netherlands is most famous for, are tulips. The Netherlands dominates world production with eighty per cent of the world market. Tulips alone account for around a third of all the bulbs produced in the Netherlands. There are over 8,530 hectares of land planted with tulip bulbs. If each bulb were planted roughly ten centimetres apart, they would circle the equator seven times!

PEOPLE *Land and the Dutch*

The Netherlands is one of the most densely populated countries in Europe. About 15.6 million people live in a country of just 41,526 square kilometres. In 2001 it had a population density of 375 people for every square kilometre. This compares with a population density of 29 people per kilometre in the United States and 243 per kilometre in the United Kingdom.

Land has always been precious in the Netherlands and, in their search for more land, the Dutch have been reclaiming land from the sea for 400 years. One of the biggest land reclamation schemes started in 1932, when an inlet from the North Sea, called the Zuider Zee, was reclaimed. A dam was built to keep out the sea and the area behind the dam was drained to make new land, known as polders MAP REF: 1 . The polders provided almost 165,000 hectares of new land for housing and agriculture. The remaining water now forms Lake Ijsselmeer, into which the Ijssel, a branch of the Rhine, drains.

Below: Amsterdam, the Netherlands' capital city, is home to a mix of races and cultures.

 **NATURE** *Windmills*

The windmill has a strong link with the Netherlands and it has played an important role in the development of the country. In the seventeenth century windmills were used to drain the low-lying land and keep it dry and habitable. The windmills used the power of the wind to turn scoops that collected water from the marshy land. The water was tipped into large tanks and fed into rivers and small streams. By the middle of the nineteenth century, there were more than 10,000 windmills in the Netherlands. Today, as electrical pumps have replaced the need for wind power, only about 1,000 remain. They are a symbol of the Dutch people's close link to water and a reminder of the skills needed to build them.

However, modern windmills, known as wind turbines, are being used more and more today. The Dutch wind energy industry is developing rapidly, mainly due to the flat, windy Dutch landscape. A single hundred-metre wind turbine can generate up to one Megawatt (MW) of electricity, enough power for up to 800 typical European households. In 2000, the Netherlands produced about 495 MW of electricity using wind turbines, which made it the seventh largest wind producer in the world. Wind energy accounts for one per cent of the Netherlands' total electricity supplies, compared to almost thirteen per cent in Denmark. But the Netherlands' share is growing fast as the Dutch seek to make more use of the flat and windy landscape. They are also developing offshore wind farms in the North Sea; they already have two close to where the Rhine meets the sea.

$ ECONOMY *Rotterdam & Europoort*

The main channel of the River Rhine (the Lek) has been widened as it nears the sea to cope with large ocean-going vessels. As we follow this channel, it takes us to Rotterdam, the world's largest port!

Rotterdam handles industrial traffic from four of Western Europe's most important economies – the Netherlands, Germany, France and Belgium. About 300 million tonnes of cargo passed through the port in 2001. That is roughly the same as one of the giant barges we've seen along the Rhine coming through the port every five minutes, every day of the year!

To cope with the huge amount of traffic using Rotterdam, a decision was made in 1957 to build an additional port, called Europoort MAP REF: 2 . Europoort was built next to the North Sea, mostly on land reclaimed from the sea. It is a state-of-the-art port with the most modern equipment and storage facilities available. As we sail towards the sea, you'll be able to see the 'disaster area'. This is where fire brigades are trained to deal with large-scale industrial accidents that could happen at the port. The complex includes a grounded tanker that is set on fire several times a day so that fire-fighters can practise their skills.

Below: Rotterdam is the world's largest port. It is crammed with ships of all shapes and sizes.

Cleaning up the river

The Rhine flows at its slowest in the delta region. As it runs out of energy most of its sediment is deposited on the river bed. The sediment contains pollutants such as chemicals and oil which have been picked up from the many industries the river has flowed past on its journey.

As the sediment builds up it can disrupt shipping and so the river has to be regularly dredged. The sediment is removed and dumped in other parts of the delta or in the North Sea. The city of Rotterdam alone has to dredge about ten million tonnes of polluted sludge from the harbour basin every year. It was estimated during the 1980s that the Rhine contributed forty per cent of the pollution in the North Sea.

Efforts have been made in recent years to reduce the amount of pollution in the delta area. One method has been to clean the sediment but this is expensive. In the 1980s, it was estimated that cleaning sediment from the Dutch part of the Rhine cost around £2.6 million a year. The Dutch have since decided that it is more cost effective (cheaper) to reduce the pollution entering the river to start with. New methods of recycling waste have been developed by industries along the river and as a result the amount of polluted sediment has been halved.

Left: Pollution from the delta area finds its way to the sea.

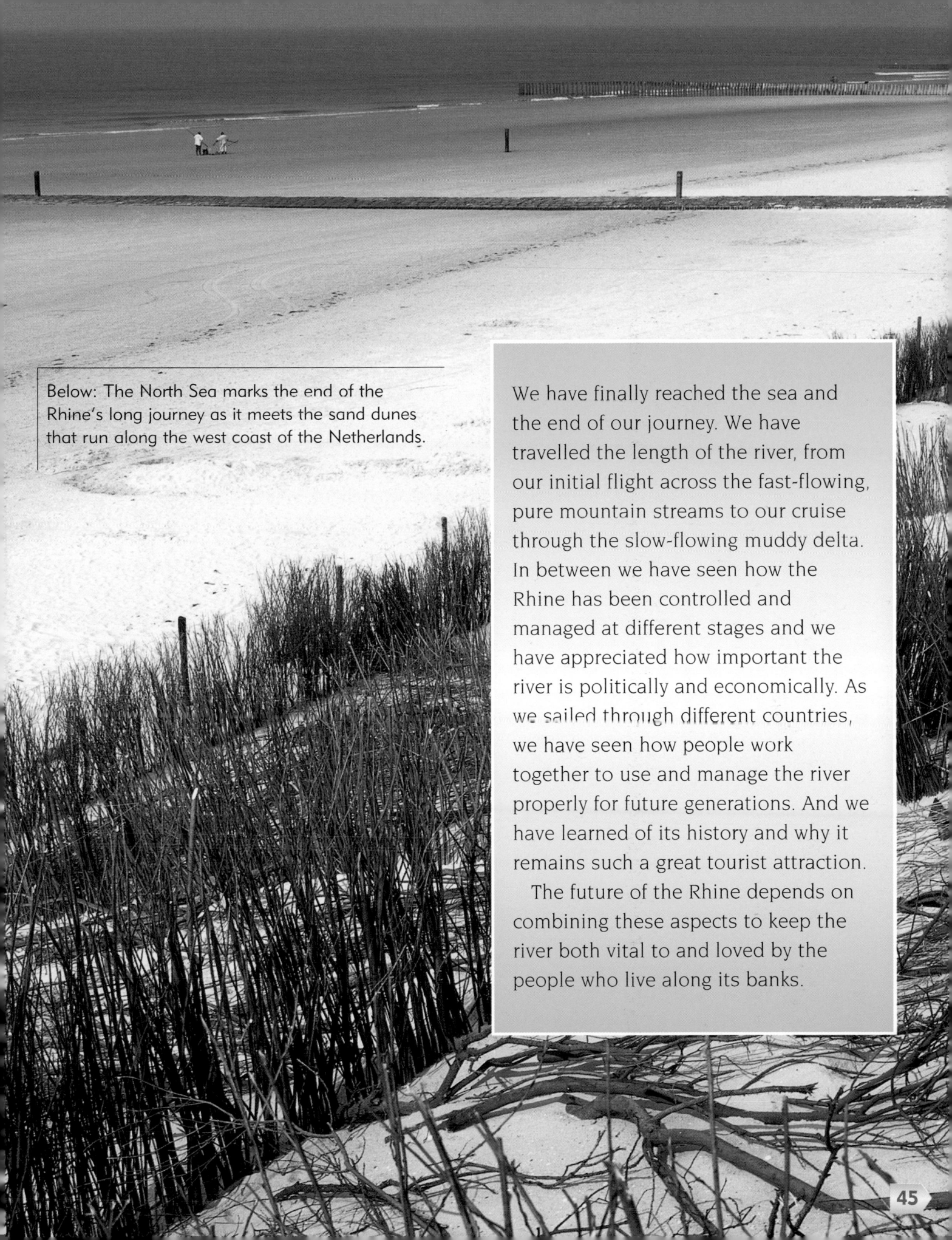

Below: The North Sea marks the end of the Rhine's long journey as it meets the sand dunes that run along the west coast of the Netherlands.

We have finally reached the sea and the end of our journey. We have travelled the length of the river, from our initial flight across the fast-flowing, pure mountain streams to our cruise through the slow-flowing muddy delta. In between we have seen how the Rhine has been controlled and managed at different stages and we have appreciated how important the river is politically and economically. As we sailed through different countries, we have seen how people work together to use and manage the river properly for future generations. And we have learned of its history and why it remains such a great tourist attraction.

The future of the Rhine depends on combining these aspects to keep the river both vital to and loved by the people who live along its banks.

From the Swiss Alps to the North Sea, the Rhine falls over 1,800 metres on its 1,320 kilometre journey.

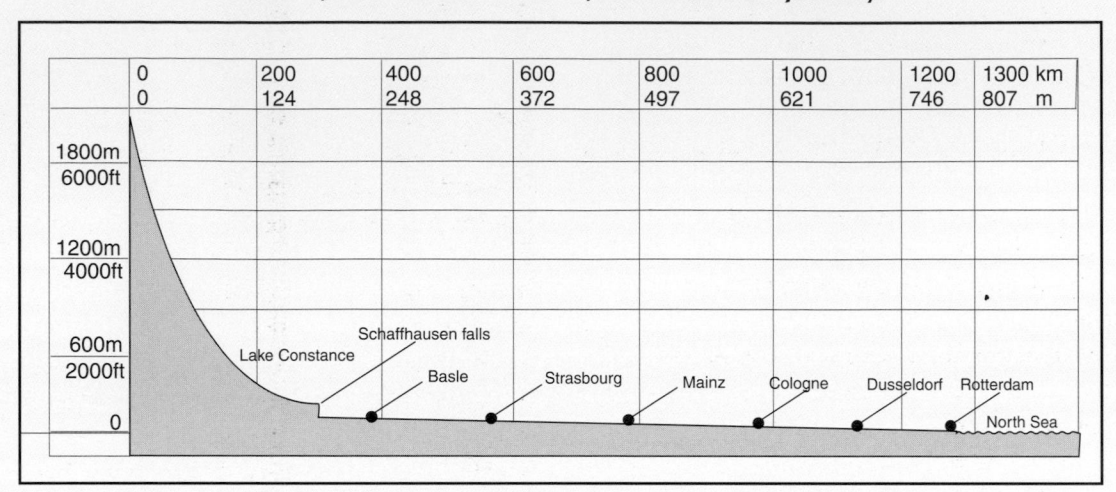

| 0 | 200 | 400 | 600 | 800 | 1000 | 1200 | 1300 km |
| 0 | 124 | 248 | 372 | 497 | 621 | 746 | 807 m |

Further Information

Useful websites

http://www.yahooligans.com/around_the_world/regions/europe/Rhine_River/

A good general site with links to general information about the river as well as some interesting photographs and facts.

http://www.factmonster.com/ce6/world/A0841717.html

Factmonster is an online information centre for young users. This address will take you directly to the Rhine River entry, but use the search function to find additional information.

Books

Great Rivers: The Rhine by Michael Pollard (Evans Brothers, 2001)

The Rhine (*Rivers of the World*) by Stuart A. Kallen (Lucent Books, 2003)

Themes in Geography: *Rivers* by Fred Martin (Heinemann Library, 1996)

Geography Fact Files: *Rivers* by Mandy Ross (Hodder Wayland, 2004)

Earth Alert! Rivers by Shelagh Whiting (Hodder Wayland, 2005)

Glossary

Alluvial From 'alluvium'. The name for any material deposited by a river.

Catchment The area drained by a river and its tributaries. The headwaters form at the edge of the catchment, then join together to make a master stream. Also known as a drainage basin.

Causeway A raised path or road over marshland or water.

Channelization To create a channel, or to direct something through a channel.

Cirque A steep, bowl-shaped hollow found at the source of a glacier.

Conurbation An extended urban area made up of a number of towns that all join together.

Delta A geographical feature at the mouth of a river, formed by the build-up of sediment.

Desalinisation The making of fresh water from sea water by removing the salt.

Downstream The direction you travel along a river when you are moving from the source to the estuary (mouth).

Dyke A long embankment used to prevent river or sea water from flooding low-lying land. In the US artificial dykes are often called 'levees'.

Erosion The wearing away of land by natural forces such as running water, glaciers, wind or waves.

Estuary An area where fresh water and salt water mix, usually found where rivers enter the sea.

Eutrophication The gradual increase in the concentration of phosphorus, nitrogen and other plant nutrients in an aging aquatic ecosystem such as a lake.

Flood When a river spills over its banks, on to land that is usually dry.

Floodplain The part of a river valley submerged during floods.

Flotilla A small fleet of ships or boats.

Glacier A large body of continuously accumulating ice and compacted snow, formed in mountain valleys or at the poles, which deforms under its own weight and slowly moves.

Gorge A deep, narrow river valley with steep, rocky sides.

Groundwater Water that is stored or moves underground in the soil or rocks.

Headwaters The streams that make up the beginning of a river.

Hydrofoil A boat with wing-like blades attached to its hull (bottom of the boat). The blades lift the boat out of the water as it increases in speed.

Landslide A sudden, rapid movement of soil or rock down a slope.

Levee A long, narrow bank that keeps the river within its channel. Levees may be natural or artificial barriers.

Meander A large bend in a river.

Meltwater Water produced by the melting of snow and ice.

Navigable Passable by ship or boat; a waterway is navigable when it is deep enough and wide enough to allow ships or boats to sail through it.

Organic farming Farming or the raising of livestock without using artificial chemicals.

Pesticides Any poison, organic or inorganic, used to destroy pests of any sort.

Polder A piece of land reclaimed from the sea, usually surrounded by dykes so that the water level can be artificially regulated.

Reservoir An artificial lake that forms when water collects behind a dam. Reservoir water may be used for irrigation or for producing hydroelectric power.

Salmon ladder A series of stepped pools through which salmon can move up a river. They jump from pool to pool until they reach the top level; they can then swim normally upstream.

Sediment Fine sand and earth that is moved and left by water, wind or ice.

Source The point at which a river begins.

Toll A tax or charge on individuals or traffic allowing them to pass a certain point.

Tributary A stream or river that flows into another larger stream or river.

Upstream The direction you travel along a river when you are moving from the estuary (mouth) back towards the source.

Waterfall A sudden fall of water over a steep drop.

Water meadow A meadow that is regularly flooded by a stream or river. Normally part of a river's floodplain.

Wetland Area of marsh or swamp where the soil is saturated with water like a sponge.

Index